FRAMED

Selected Poetry 1974 - 2000

Helen DW Humphries

SEABANK

This paperback edition published in Great Britain by **SEABANK** in 2021

© Helen DW Humphries 2021

Helen DW Humphries has asserted her moral right to be identified as the Author of this work in accordance with the Copyright, Design and Patents Act 1988.

All rights reserved, including the right of reproduction in whole or in part in any form. Copyright under Berne Convention.
A CIP record for this title is available from the British Library.

ISBN 978-1-9997978-1-2

Typeset in Minion Pro by Kerrie Moncur Design and Typesetting
kmdesigntypesetting@outlook.com

Cover design by Kerrie Moncur
Cover image 102226054 © creativecommonsstockphotos | Dreamstime.com
Author photograph by Erdmute Underwood

Printed and bound by Bell & Bain, Glasgow

Helen DW Humphries
Framed

SEABANK
Seabank,
Turnberry Road,
Maidens,
Ayrshire,
KA26 9NN

SEABANK is committed to sustainable sourcing.
This book is made from Forest Stewardship Council® certified paper

MIX
Paper from responsible sources
FSC
www.fsc.org FSC® C007785

to James

CONTENTS

Foreword	ix
Acknowledgements	xiii
FRAMED	1
SLEEP	2
AT THE EDGE OF THE SEA	3
ANGORA SWEATER	4
TO KEATS	5
BITTER LEMON PEEL	6
KNITTING	7
STRANDS OF MY LIFE	8
SPEECHLESS IN BED	12
COUPLES	13
AVEBURY	14
WE WERE ONLY JOKING	15
HOUSE	16
SEA-SHANTY	17
THE ST. LOUIS ARCH	18
STONE	19
CÉIDE FIELDS	20
CROAGH PATRICK	21

FRAMED

A NEW TREATMENT FOR PUFFY EYES	22
FELLOW TRAVELLER	23
A PASCHAL PRAYER	24
HEART OF MIDLOTHIAN	25
FORVIE SANDS	26
VISITOR	27
TO JIMMY ON THE TRAIN	28
LEAP YEAR	29
FEMININE ENDINGS	30
TOO BUSY TO TALK	31
DESICCATION	32
SINGAPORE	33
DUNDAFF FALLS	34
GIRVAN	35
OFF THE CIRCUIT	37
AT THE SAVOY	38
NYC	39
MUM	41
BOOSEY & HAWKES (REGENT STREET)	42
GOOD, BAD AND MARRIED	43
COCKTAILS	44
WHERE DO YOU GO?	46
YTHAN ESTUARY	47
G AND T	48
TALK TO ME	49
SACRED GEOMETRY	50

FOREWORD
Framed: the Poetry of Helen DW Humphries: An Appreciation

This is a powerful first collection. Here in particular are vivid shards of a woman's experience, written with a 'word-edged knife' and an ear for the vernacular. The poems are particularly 'giving' on 'emotional matters.' Creative writing may provide personal testimony, but there is a constant mix of recall and imagination. While there is much good observation from the 'wartime' front (of what used to be called the 'battle of the sexes'), there is also a 'taking stock', meditations on love and passing time. Yet the poems also celebrate the moment, the loves and relationships that affirm and warm us. This is a story told honestly about the pleasure and pains (and later reflections) of a woman who 'Loves and gives.'

There is humour, but in the more ambitious poems there is more at stake – a coming to terms. We have lost loves, and how the everyday and the 'taken for granted' became, all too quickly, matters of memory. Parallel to these themes is a sensitivity to nature and place, and to echoes of historical traumas felt in the presence of monuments, both natural and man-made. The recall is vivid and resonant, especially when a series of lines catch alight, or explode like squibs. The personal stories are often given broader significance by reference to the mysteries of 'ancestral folk,' to the wisdom of those who have gone before. Celtic scenes are particularly mined.

Boyfriends and lovers are subject to scrutiny as they jet off and away, or call 'remotely' from across the globe, or who seem unable to conceive that they might be given 'some news' (*Talk to Me*). In various ways they place their own career and self-fulfilment first, and leave a wound. Many of the poems are reflections on relationships in the past, but to look back is also to engage with the future.

FRAMED

We learn, in tightly wrought poems that often burst into a super-resonance, and accelerate. We get vivid reportage, wry humour, and sadness. We hear of the rituals, and the snares and delusions, but also of what is left behind, the lingering fire of love. These are warm, positive verses, even when the feelings foreshadow regret and (occasionally) self-blame and anger. We hear of a young son's musings (travelling on a train), but also of the fleeting images of him **in** a windowsill picture frame – beyond capture and permanence (*To Jimmy on the Train, Framed*). Winter recurs, with all its darker associations, but the tone is generally affirmative. There are 'selfish men', but this is not a book of bitterness; *Fellow Traveller*, for example, tells of the warming and distracting conviviality of a scoundrel – again on a train. When love works it affirms life, and also beats the age-cheating balms of the beauty counter (*A New Treatment for Puffy Eyes*). There is startling economy and precision: the closing double metaphors in *St Louis Arch*, and (in *Céide Fields*) a man who 'plants' and departs, or disappears. There are moving and touching tributes – especially in *Mum* – although that poem toughly asserts the primacy of the living in our concern, and reminds us of one who was born a 'tiger not a lamb'. The work on an 'unfulfilled sweater' (in *Knitting*) is also both beautifully observed, and touching.

The moments I mention – an insider's testimony – often hang on a few key lines that bring a climax, at beginning, middle or end. We hear of marrying a 'limpet', for example – a brilliant image in a 'story' of marriage and release (*Sea-shanty*). Past is present we are always told, and here the poet is a soldier at the front, in the war of love – constantly sensitive to messages and residues from those who went before; the mystical and the everyday are in constant play.

The collection is full of pleasures, not all of them (as is right) delivered on first readings: a revelry on sleep (*Sleep*); a meditation on the thrill of youthful seaside love (*At the Edge of the Sea*); a take on time and decay (*To Keats*); a short and brilliant poem on taking rugged hold of life (*Bitter Lemon Peel*). I like the longer *Strands of My Life* too ('I seized the flower', recalling Wordsworth), with its sparkling word-play, and lyrical conceit of weaving life's threads. I was moved by *House*, while *Céide Fields* combines love, messages from the 'ancient folk', and the natural world ('Peat seams … pierced through by black bogwood'): the personal and the observational, with hints of the epic. There is great fun to be had here too (the wonderfully and self-consciously over the top *Good, Bad and Married*, for example, and *Boosey & Hawkes (Regent Street)*).

Foreword

Not all the poems are equally good, as you would expect. Some provide moments and passages of observation, and themes, which are not perhaps sustained. I think the more ambitious work is the most resonant. One thinks of the very personal *Sacred Geometry*, and of *Ythan Estuary*, where an almost pantheist feel for nature also suggests something of a philosophy for later life, beyond revelries of 'magic days.' I also love the rawness of *Desiccation* – a story of a Saturday's child after Saturday has passed. There are wry, even cynical reflections on being a couple, even being a kind of high roller for a time - of ruses and deceptions. But always there is a return to feeling, and to truths that last.

Many will enjoy and gain much from this (long awaited) collection.

Brian Neve

Author of: *Film and Politics in America: A Social Tradition* (1992); *"Un-American" Hollywood: Politics and Film in the Blacklist Era* (joint editor, 2007); *Elia Kazan: the Cinema of an American Outsider* (2009); *The Many Lives of Cy Enfield: Film Noir, The Blacklist, and Zulu* (2015).

August 2021.

ACKNOWLEDGEMENTS

I should like to thank Frances Brown and Derek Hall for their initial selection of poems for this volume. Derek has been invaluable as editor, and as producer of calm!

Many thanks to Bill Arnott for his initial cover designs and ideas.

'Sleep' was first published in *Pieces of Eight* (Aberdeen University Press, 1978).

'Speechless in Bed' was previously published in the Girvan and District Writing Group's (2019) *An Anthology*.

'Heart of Midlothian' and 'Forvie Sands' first appeared in the *Aberdeen University Review 1994*.

'Girvan' was previously published in *Crazy Jane* (Clark University Press, 1982).

'Ythan Estuary' first appeared in *Aberdeen University Review 1996*.

FRAMED

*A little boy smiles at me
From pictures on the windowsill.
He grew into the bigger picture
On my dressing-table.*

*We held hands and declared war
In the cellar.
We laughed and pulled each other's
Hair.
Tears smudged dirt on our faces together.*

*A little boy grew up with me
And was always there.
Only, he grew quicker than I,
And walked out of his images
On the dressing-table
And the windowsill.*

SLEEP

Sink softly into
Silken shades of night.
Rest your shallow head,
Hot against cool dreams, and
Sleep.

Rooftops of woods open skylights
To the stars and
Nightless gods draw curtains on your
Eyes.

Spill into unseen
Fountains, sprinkling
Lullaby fantasies
On mind's rock.
Splash and spray.

Rest warm.
Pillow-pummel in
Feather-plumed
Sleep.

AT THE EDGE OF THE SEA

When sea-salt mingled on the shore
With summer sun, we loved—no more
Nor less than that. Our lives were thrilled
With swimming where the blueness spilled.

When cloudless skies deepened to black
And evening drew the country back
To regions of ethereal calm,
We slumbered, breathing lover's balm.

The children played, away from school
In morning, in the restless cool.
At mid-day even would they stay
To burn the moment of their day.

And we would lie on grass or sand
To feel the sun fulfil the land.
Never did we think too long
That summer soon would end its song.

But now the sea-salt in the waves
Has crystallised where sunshine fades.
The tides are changing on the shore
In autumn winds—we love no more

Nor less than that.

For we may mouth with whitened lips,
While winter's world is trapped in drifts
And icy water hits the edge,
Our silent, deadened, lover's pledge.

ANGORA SWEATER

Lockerbie and Lancaster
Separated by a painful road to Penrith.
The train hurtles through snow, while
"The Plough Inn"
Beckons in early morning grey
To Passengers who cannot
Disembark, though they may want to.

Soft,
In a Christmas-given
Angora sweater,
She hangs limply
From the waist,
Where her lover's
Arms hold.

Couched,
In an uncomfortable
Train seat,
They warm against
Steamed windows:
The countryside
Sleets past.

From Scotland
To England,
It is winter.

TO KEATS

Mind's time is striving to nurture the hours
When faces are formed by imagining powers.
The hands on the clock will not cease to run
Through seconds and minutes of timing the sun.

And quietly the books on the shelves will decay
Dusty, and crusted, in hiding from day.
Silently, too, in foreseeing its death,
The heart will constrain its own pensive breath.

Mind's self is striving to harvest an age,
Where feeling and thinking unite on the page.
The volumes of soul that are still left unread
Are merely assumed to be dying, or dead.

And gently the heart of the mind will imply,
It cannot conceive of its having to die,
Before it has known that its efforts to feel
Were regarded as beauty, and thought to be real.

Feathers are lifting to winnow the air:
Driftingly fragile, escaping from where
Their fineness is forming an integral part
Of purity—born and conceived in the heart.

BITTER LEMON PEEL

Take this lemon,
And cut it
Sharply through with a
Word-edged knife.

Squeeze the juice
And drink the bitter
Cold in a glass, seen
Through by everyone.

Lastly, not to waste the
Chance—roughly rub
The tender, yellow skin,
Hard, against the grater.

KNITTING

I started knitting a jumper
For you once.
But in a few months
"You" had changed.
I didn't know what to do.

So, it remained unknitted
And unpurled:
There it was,
The unfulfilled sweater.

I braced myself and
Began again this woolly part
For another heart.
I thought,
"Will the old pattern fit,
If I finish it?"

But it didn't.

STRANDS OF MY LIFE

*There is always a time of night
When I know that my life is not right,
That it has no plot,
No true characterisation,
No conclusions in the thought.*

*I get up early, catch the train,
Return alone at night again.*

*All the while, during
This easy repetition
Of seeming order,
I am missing you, and friends from old,
And feel, perhaps, I sold
Myself down the river,
And made a mistake.*

*That is, too early
I employed myself
In emotional matters:
The boyfriends, sweethearts,
Lovers and
Divorced paters.*

*I seized the flower.
The blooms all died.
I watched them wilt
At my side.*

So, where to now?
I like all the rest,
Can only keep trying my best,
Higher still aiming,
Without blaming
Too much my self
For the casual ruin
Of belief.

It would not suit me
To want to
Dwell on grief.

There is an idealistic goal
Preening itself behind my acts,
Although you have thought,
"She sees through cataracts."

Blindness, only,
Could make this woman
Fail to live as you would wish.
For a start, she does not earn
Or seem to learn
Much.

Far better, then, to quit,
To leave off thought of "It".

I do not promise any
A life of quiet content:

The blissful afternoons spent in
Reading,
Weeding,
Cooking,
Looking on in happy love.
The strands need a weaver,
A perceiver,
A believer.
One who intertwines
With colourful vision
A tableau, fit to hang
Upon a wall:
Not too high,
Certainly not low.
Someone who knows
Where the light will shine
Just so,
To make the most of
Contrasting light and shade.

But that someone must be I,
For I have half the picture made.

The rest must simply wait.
I must find the time
To place the strands where I want them.

The would-be weavers will not do for this tapestry.
I have discovered in my freer moments,
They are all deceivers.
I share the art

With only a few
Whom I can trust.

It is hard to tell someone
Impeccable as you,
Quite where the threads
Did not hold,
Or
When it was the canvas
Burst.
The loose ends meet,
Ravel and knot.
We encounter one another
Off and on,
Here and there,
Now and then.
But still,
The same question:
Why can it not be perfect?

I elect you.
You choose me.
We, nevertheless
Cannot be.

SPEECHLESS IN BED

Last night I went to bed
Without the art of conversation.
It doesn't waken up beside me
Any more.

This has happened before.
After a few days—
(Or, if I'm lucky, weeks)—
My man takes my art of conversation
And makes love with it
In another's story,
Leaving me

Speechless in bed.

COUPLES

While I am dancing here,
You are conversing there.
No-one really knows us
As two parts of a pair.

At parties we've agreed
To separate our ways:
Being seen together socially
Was fine in fonder days.

Instead we like to be around
And giving points of view,
To people who mean nothing much—
To either me or you.

AVEBURY

Chill hoar frosts sunshine. Scalpel-fine wind
Fliters bleak and blear and loamy land,
Where centuries revise themselves amid stark,
Monolithic giants, who stand, hurl back
Through decades of an arcane world, a
Quiet and looming ghostliness.

What is to blame I cannot name the feeling,
Wrought by a ditch, drawing pitch black
Silhouettes from the pallor of the past?

I wish, I wish I could know what life meant to
These petrified phantoms, how dear to them
The Wiltshire landscape!

But I cannot.

Buried still with the threatening snow,
They whisper only in voices I may
Never know, never hear.

WE WERE ONLY JOKING

I only called to ask if you were having an affair.
Of course, I couldn't have known at the time,
She was right there.
Or, that when you said, "No,"
You had placed me this low on your list of pleasures.

Well, now I take my own measures to make me feel
   better.
Also, thanks for your letter, which meant something
   at the time,
But was presumably, just a joke, a callous
   calculation on your part
To placate me, keep me hoping, hanging on as if
   there was something
To look forward to:
I thought it was you.

I hope you will share the joke with those who
   already laughed,
And tell them, too, that
The one day you bothered to come home
(only to catch a flight the very next night)
You pulled out the straw
Which hurt the camel's back.

Nay, isn't the proverb that it
"Broke"?
And here's the joke:
I anticipated more,
But not this sore,
Dull, hurtful pain
Of knowing you can
Never do this to me again.

HOUSE

I have a new house.
The house is mine.
In three months,
Everything has changed.
I hate the deranged way things happen.

I have no love.
No love is mine.
Nothing has changed.
I hate the deranged way things happen.

No-one knows what we said or did, that made me
    bid
For loneliness and pain: that subject again.
I was writing that when you were around.
Now there is no sound, except the sobbing flurry of
    heating,
Which I cannot pay for, and the writing, which will
    not pay me.
We'll see.

I'm tired and seem so full of hate tonight.
But, it is late, and you are about to disappear on a
    plane again.
The world is so full of selfish men.
I can count one hundred and ten thousand between
    me and you.
It's true.

You are in that line of men,
Travelling on a road to self-fulfillment without me.
I am lonely in my house, but my heart bleeds for
    you.
It's true.

SEA-SHANTY

If I'd wanted to be a nun, a nun,
I would have been a nun.
But that would not have been much fun for me,
Would not have been fun for me.

Instead I married, I married,
I foolishly married
A limpet, fished out of the sea for me,
Fished out of the sea for me.
It was always shut tight, shut tight all night,
And would never open for me,
Would never open for me.

One wintry day, one wintry day,
Why I cannot say,
I shook myself from the marriage bed
And took my shell to the beach, to the beach,
I took my shell to the beach.

With cool head, with very cool head,
I threw, I threw, I threw
Old limpet, limpet into the sea,
As far as I could reach.

The tide came in, the tide came in
Limpet couldn't swim for me.
He couldn't swim, and I don't blame him,
I don't blame him, I blame me.
I don't blame him, I blame me.

THE ST. LOUIS ARCH

Gateway to the West, arched in hopeful fire,
White silver against a brooding black sky of
Dark blame and desire.

Lurched from an architect's hauling page,
Planned to convey earth to heaven
While the rivers rise with rage.

Winter of floods disproves promise of old:
A rainbow-shadowing myth
Whose banks are too ancient to hold.

Standing, a hover
Above our teeming life:
A wishbone, arch of the feast,

Leftover.

STONE

*Conversation hangs as ice from rock.
Our souls are etched in stone:
Winter mocks an Autumn day,
When you say anything*

To me.

*Each, loving, comes upon the same.
Your words leave me alone:
Spring beckons Winter away,
When you say anything*

To me.

*Solitude stares like a ghost from dreams.
My heart cannot condone:
Summer comes to those who may*

To me.

CÉIDE FIELDS

You call from sunny Australia,
As unreal but true as a dream,
Your voice surprising my silence:
"I was thinking—what might have been."

And I shamble on in the furrows of
The sodden and high Céide Fields,
Determined to maintain my balance,
In shock at what is revealed.

Peat seams are pierced through by black bogwood,
Arms outstretched as in horrible crime,
Boughs dismembered and gruesomely buried
By five thousand years of abandoning time.

In the midst of weird, natural beauty,
As wild and rich as my soul,
I curse the place that you left for,
Its dry warmth usurping my role.

For just as this ancient folk toiled here,
Then disappeared quite from the cliffs,
You planted, worked, then left me,
Alive in a grave of grief.

You call from sunny Australia,
As unreal but true as a dream,
Your voice surprising my silence:
"I was thinking what might have been."

My progress next is in Thunder,
On Croagh Patrick—the pilgrims' hill,
With your words blowing loud all around me,
'Til I know that I love you still.

CROAGH PATRICK

*Dark, and green, a hill. The presence of a saint
  unseen,
To whom souls trudge, and from whom souls have
  flown:
It is no wonder that you were unknown to us, still
  foreigners
In our own souls' land.*

*At your feet, the meet and solemn memorial for a
  people gone—
The bronze and seemly ship—that took them from a
  land torn
By yet more foreigners.*

*Now light and rain, one day. The loving of a pair
  surprised
To be pilgrims, too. Suspecting each moment upon a
  sigh or smile:
It may not last. But cast a glance at human dance
  and feel
Upon the road, we are in step.*

*You, with your injured leg, and I, with my damaged
  heart
Could not look upon this Mayo scene and stay long
  apart.*

*The rainbows on Inis Mor ask us to pour ourselves
  backwards
And forwards, seeking the great store of spirit blasted
Upon the cliffs and rocks at Dun Angus. God asks
  for us
To memorise the scudding skies and happy sands
Where we ran amid cries of gulls and birds, we
  could not name.*

A NEW TREATMENT FOR PUFFY EYES

Tell Harvey Nix to keep their girls
Gelled, lotioned, cleansed and pure
At their ground-floor, gorgeous-face counters:
Tell them not to sell me any more.

I have worked out what it takes
To keep my face, even if it ages:
It is not an easy notion, and involves
Many queasy stages.

First, you have to be over forty
And smoke, and drink, despite what
The girls at the Clarins counter think.
Then, you have to get up late,
Feeling on the brink.

Rub under the eyes, with nothing more than a cold,
    damp cloth.
Use running water, engage the Clinique girls in
    wrath.
Have a cup of coffee—toxins disallowed on the
    face-treatment floor—
And wait, and then, know a true love is knocking at
    your door.

Nauseating, isn't it, and priceless?
I'm chucking out my potions, and all the lotions, for
    being ageless.
I'm growing old with him, and glad.
Unlike the latest absolute skin-recovery care from
    Lancôme,
This is not a fad!

FELLOW TRAVELLER

The winter is here: a winter that knows no dawn.
My commuting friend is placed as a pawn in prison.
I do not know if it is right that he has embezzled,
As charged, overnight, such vast sums.

The winter is here: a winter that knows no dawn.
He has asked for more of everything, the man who
    would be king.
But he informed our journeys with such conviviality,
It was easy to see that we were forgiving of his talk of
Riches and splendid living: he dispelled the tedium
    of our journeying,
And was our fellow traveller.

The winter is here. It is only dawning on me, how
    severe.

A PASCHAL PRAYER

*The church flowers flare in blinding white and
   yellow—the
Horticultural hues of innocence and hope.
And all reflect and reinvest arched stone with mellow
Sun, enlightening through the spiritual scope.
One woman waits patiently aside,
Her private apparition not yet devised.
The sermon starts her Easter Day:
"What," ask our souls, "do we need the most:
Spring lamb with rosemary, or the resurrected
   Christ?"*

*It's not all chocolate eggs, and cards, though maybe
   lamb so rare.
It's the way that woman looked so hard, into the cave,
   in tears,
And he wasn't there...
It's the pain for our sin, it's the violence of bloody fear.
It's the rolling away of the stone, it's an angel standing
   there.
It's the agony of a mother and son, it's the face of a
   Father unknown,
It's the frightened knocking on his door.
And the woman asks, "What if he's not in?"*

*England's apple-trees blossom, blithely fair.
Blackbirds nest and church bells peal.
The spring lambs skip in fields so dear.
One woman kneels patiently aside,
Her own vision not yet devised,
Her whispering prayer, close enough to feel,
"After that darksome night, let this light be real."*

HEART OF MIDLOTHIAN

If star-strewn fortune in time unkindly beat
A staggering descent from Arthur's Seat;
If, from blackening Salisbury Crags, Southwest you
     found
A widening Wiltshire landscape, fold you around;
I call you back, where as a child, you wandered free.
A north Venetian world fastened your hand on me.

Abroad, fantasy-peddlers at market stalls
Held you in spiced and aromatic thrall.
Warm oceans of love in blue-white flame
Lapped on your shores of drug-eyed blame.

No volcanic rocks in thistled haar,
With strengthening skies and keening cloud,
Rouse you from sleep to roll a tear,
And yearn my cobbled mile with vennels proud.

FORVIE SANDS*

The sands at Forvie do not lie, except upon some souls
Of fisherfolk, whose names we know in books from long ago.
Their eyes are sand, their bones are weed, our footsteps tread upon.
Our spirits hear the ghosts alive, though they are long forlorn.

The North Sea pounds within our hearts, and harsh against the shore.
Sun winter-brights, the day is short, our voices sing for more.
Your gaze is far, your thoughts are near, the sounds are not our own.
They come away, with history, and buried tales between.

This is the first I bear my breast to earthly wind and cold.
You are aghast, this foreign lass can make herself so bold.
To you, not them, though all the same, though all the same at last.
I dig for you, sandcastles make, and sing the songs of past.

At Forvie Sands, I loved you then, I saw the nets swing wide:
The North Sea gave a mindful wave to fleshy legs in stride.
You are my man, as far we can, as far the oceans give
The memory of Forvie Sands to those who died, and live.

*The village of Forvie, on the North East coast of Scotland, was once a thriving fishing community, buried by shifting sand dunes in a storm of 1413.

VISITOR

There is a gleaning of light through my dark door.
I have obstructed it, thrown gallons of dimming
Wine and inanimate spirit to ban its presence;
Depressed its luminous joy with sad and mournful
Tales of what fails in my life.
(Why am I no-one's wife, since I sparkle,
Once gave joie-de-vivre?)

This light has crept in, importing
To my craving and desperate mind that
The goal is not a solitude to grieve, but a solitude to
Give and have and remember: to love, to be mindful,
To be kind.

Today, the light shone through, blearily, at my back door.
I have tried, unsuccessfully, but from now, will make
    myself ask for more.
It was not God, but one of his ain folk: a little angel,
Who appeared and told me, as if for a joke:
"To love yourself is also to love them."

If I may share a little of this beam, only young and
Knocking still, not quite let-in:
Then, will you think it a sin that I have tried
To maintain the early-morning glimpses of dawn,
Mention to people who were always busy and other-
    wise-occupied,
That the colour of skies might have influenced them,
But the colour of sky dulled for me on my own?

It is hard to know of oneself that a place can be grey,
    if alone.

TO JIMMY ON THE TRAIN

The sun on fire-setting,
West from this Swindon-gaining train,
The moon above Wiltshire's White Horse
Window-through-appearing and
A son beside me, fatigued from his London-daying,
Asks if a string is attached between them,
The Sun and the Moon:

"Does the one going down
Pull the other up?"

If this is true,
As he grows up,
Must I grow down?

I hope before then to light
The world awhile with him.

LEAP YEAR

In the dark, the ripples cease,
The River Thames flows past.
Our bodies warm, at peace.

Sailors, explorers, lightermen –
Centuries beyond our ken –
Sigh soul-songs through the night.

At first light in bed it is
A leap year date to
Ask you to marry me:

You say, "I might get a better offer.
We'll see."

Leaving you.
Walking under Tower Bridge,
I ache for its poise, its span.
Knowing for that brief moment:
Only you can.

You might get a better offer.
I still have love to last, watching
The River Thames flow past.

You and I have the souls of
Sailors, explorers, lightermen –
Centuries beyond our ken.

FEMININE ENDINGS

In France, they have them for all things small.
If you're an "-ette", I'll bet
You've slept with my man.
Which one doesn't matter.
My love-life has been shattered
By diminutive endings:
The secret surrenderings of
*Dian**a**, Pau**line**, Annab**elle**, or Yv**ette**.*
All of them living up to their names,
Playing little girls' rules in big men's games.

What's more maddening for me at least
Is that, once in Greece,
I was taken quite pleasantly off for a swim
By a gorgeous young thing (enough of him),
And only later realising
My attraction was (not surprising) not me,
But that my name in Greek had to be
Attributed with an "-a" for a while.

Not liking the style, I departed to seek a man
Not so unbending, so easily charmed by a
Feminine ending.

TOO BUSY TO TALK

"Look, darling, I have to go to a meeting."
"That's alright, it's just a quick greeting: how are you?"
"I don't have time. Can I call you back, and we'll make a plan?"
"If you have to, but I wanted to tell you about this other man."

DESICCATION

I tried very hard to stay
The way I was at twenty-one:
Full of life and fun,
"Loving and giving"—
A Saturday's child.

After ten years and more of living,
And becoming a mother,
I am foreign to myself,
Become a stranger, another.

I look older than I am.
It was all a scam of
Short-lived fantasy,
That dirty dream of staying me.

They fade away, the early players.
Now only the disbelieving stares
Of my grey-haired allies
Who watch my otiose rebellion in surprise.

Nicotine and alcohol are the only medication
For my ripeningly total desiccation.

SINGAPORE

I am driven away from my wife
By business deals in
Singapore and Hong Kong.
Tonight I dine in L.A. with a friend I met in London.
She and I eat oysters, drink champagne and
Have the fun my wife suspects me of having.
She and I talk about her latest job; my wife,
Who said this morning she is leaving; and,
The kids.

Soft, this skin, just arrived from Dallas,
To drive to Mexico, while I fly tomorrow for Singapore.

She picks me up and drops me at the airport.
We love each other, but it is easy to part.
Our context is fantasy and fulfilment.
Reality plays a minor role in our relationship.

It is easy to part.

Yet, as she pulls out into the L.A. traffic,
Having kissed me,
I wonder at how she will cope with the drive ahead,
And, at how I will carry my baggage without
Her help.

DUNDAFF FALLS

Like straw on the floor,
Lightening the room with every shaft
Of sunlight through the window, a door
Left open, the walls shining bright:
Are you or I the reflector, and which is the light?

The hills hang yellow and green
With mists rolling over them.
Occasionally, the scream of some
Silver-armoured, mutilated soldier
Livens the silence of years,
and
Stillness, when war was fought.
Clashing, crashing tumbling in our ears of
Where the river falls and hate is grown over by love
And peace is endlessly wrought.

Fish fliver and rill in the raith where
Visions like these run us in tears.

GIRVAN

The heart has struggled with the sun and
Battled with its moon moods
To make you love in storms and
Floods of rain.
Spilling, gushing, seasoned
Thought disappears
Under wet, shiny roadsides
To find the sea—
At your childhood harbour
Where boats are still rocking
To the water's wave rhythms.

I think that you knew
More than felt pleasure at the
Dark edge, where fishermen spat.
You wandered into tides,
Coming and going at the unprepared
Moments of melancholy,
The nets and smell of seaweed
Tangled your memory forever,
So that when you are exiled
From your child's heart, you
Cannot escape hearing
The seagull's cry tearing
At you above the sore lowdown of the shows—
Candy-floss, ice-cream, fish
And chips, toffee-apples—
Also at the harbour mouth.

*The seagull sang to you then,
But in your young bed your head
Lay nearly asleep and the
White-winged majesty paused outside your window,
Suspended,
Until you answered him
In childish soft breathing,
Until he knew you would go with him,
Some day, out of your hard, restless dreaming.*

OFF THE CIRCUIT

Epistolary friends we've become.
What else, when everything
But my writing hand and mind
Is numb?
I laughed in retrospect with the poem you sent,
At the familiar, niggling regret of flying too often,
At the scheduled neglect of a heart wanting softened.

But it's not the same, is it?
Months altered the artless confidence
With which we boarded planes and trains.
Each time I step towards London
I think of you in transit and
Know that, although appearance might belie the
    thought,
The same travelling buccaneer you are not.

Nor I. But I had changed before you,
And this isn't about me. I still see
You flying with success and know you
Don't want redress of anything before, though
There's a greater depth to your lore.
Still a glittering eye or intelligent muse
Might present on the way to somewhere.

But the brief entertainment always has pause:
For me, when I wish you were there.

AT THE SAVOY

The turn of your cheek
Against mine is hot.
Men in suits, men in ties,
Women smoking cigarettes,
Make-up on their eyes.

Restless shifting, about to fly.
You want my love. I give it.
Men at work, men at play.
Women longing languidly,
Frustrated at their day.

You've nearly flown. We tarry.
We sit and sip and sigh.
Men in love, men in marriage.
Women sitting shyly,
Ready for the barrage

Of questions. I'm asking you:
"Are you a man, shy, ready,
Suited, tied, made-up, playing,
Longing, sitting, sipping, sighing,
Married?"

NYC

Above Manhattan, this
Great-bellied bird emulates
The Trojan Horse,
Concealing infiltrators.
Homeric phrases fly back, of
Proud Paris, Hector, Menelaus and
Foolish fights for
One great dame,
Whose life was naught
Without her warriors.

Her name, my name.

No battles fought for me. Though,
I sojourn in a new world and
Thrill to hear the clamour of
Old Troy ring back in
Loud, American paradox.

New York's pillars, still standing.
Yankee Stadium resounding with the chorus of
Adulation for its gladiators,
While Troy ceases in mythological somnolence.
Traditions of Trojan valour forgotten,
Sighted occasionally in home runs,
Flood-lit arenas, and thousands,
Hungry for heroism.

Troy decays, America plays.
Manhattan beckons underworld.
Beyond, New York State spins
Memories of Spartan years, spent with
My Menelaus and his godless children.

Enthralled as Helen was, my visitations to
Ithaca, Troy, Syracuse told me:
Antiquity has come to rest in upstate
New York.
My Menelaus and I,
Distant now as
Central Park and Mount Olympus.
Centuries have passed between
Helen's wars and mine.

MUM

Let it be about hope, not despair.
Let it be about us, who are here, not there.

Let us remember those who are gone.
Let our stillness harmonise a present song.
I love you, too, with my heart and life:
You are my mother, and my father's wife.
Do not go down to the cellar yet,
For it is dark, and cold, and dank and wet.

I need you, too,
Like a babe of your womb. I am who I am.
Understand, though, for it is true:
You gave birth to a tiger, not a lamb.

Let it be about hope, not despair.
Let it be about us, who are here, and who care.

BOOSEY & HAWKES
(REGENT STREET)

Don't forget
Your clarinet.
Don't leave it on the plane.
Don't forget
Your clarinet:
It bears a funny name.

Don't refuse
Your Scottish muse.
Don't leave her high and dry.
Don't refuse
Your Scottish muse.
She'll love you by and by.

Don't regret
The time you've spent
Enjoying all she has.

Don't forget
Your clarinet.
Don't leave it on the plane.
Don't forget
Your clarinet:
It bears a funny name.

GOOD, BAD AND MARRIED

*You're my honey-lipped and honey-dipped
North-of-the-border Arctic dove.
You're my economic, academic,
Intellectual love.
You're my Scotch-drinking man of mystery.*

Are you happy to be bad and mad with me?

*You're my letter-writing, window-brightening,
Golf-playing desire.
You're my sex-oozing, champagne-boozing
Filament of fire.
You're my heavy-breathing man of fantasy.*

Are you happy to be bad and mad with me?

*You're my double-cream, wet dream,
Super-cool ice-lolly.
You're the captain of my football team.
You've knocked me off my trolley.
You're the full string section of my symphony.*

Are you happy to be bad and mad with me?

*You're my milk of human kindness,
You're the opening of my eyes.
You're my harvesting of riches,
You're the parting of my thighs.
You're my pleasure, you're my treasure,
You're my hope beyond compare.
You're married: do I care?*

Are you happy to be bad and mad with me?

COCKTAILS

I know the comfort of
Green, red, dark walls,
Expensive, leather chairs and
Perfumes of international affluence.

I know the racy bars of New York, Boston, San
    Francisco and L.A.
I know all this, how can I say, because I am a woman
Who knows the need for company, the next drink,
    the careless cocktail
That induces illusion, delusion, confusion and rejection.

Whatever the bar, they all leave together,
Leaving me unknown, alone.

I know how to fend off the advances of overweight
    businessmen,
Cool the fervour of the talkative, tourist, shopping,
    lunching lady.
I know how to stare back at the boys who would
    brawl beside me,
Untouched and untouching.

I know how to befriend the bartenders, how to seem
As if I am waiting for someone, when I am not.
I know how to catch the train I nearly forgot, and
    don't remember,
How to appear resident at the hotel, how to feign
    being unwell.
How to listen and not hear, how to hear and not
    learn.

I know the dreary, non-smoking lunch with a bunch
    of tea-totallers, how to
Make an excuse to go early, somewhere after, and
    then,
That door opens again. I can plan a quick snort in
    any resort.
It leaves me untogether,
Leaves me unknown and alone.

I like the green, red, dark walls,
Which cause my falls.
I know they will give me comfort.

WHERE DO YOU GO?

"Where do you go when you leave me,
Is it far to the place to deceive?
Do you care when you're gone that I feel so withdrawn
And my heart and my soul cannot breathe?"

"I go nowhere far, and wherever you are,
Remember my arms are around you.
The touch of your skin keeps my love well within
The embrace which we shared upon parting."

"I do not know how, but the sweat from my brow
And the heat of my breasts cannot say,
How the light in my life darkens deep into night,
When I watch as you turn on your way."

"I do not go far, and wherever you are,
Remember my strong arms surround.
The warmth of your thighs strengthens our deep
    love's fires.
I won't wander too far off today."

"But what of tomorrow, next week, or next year?"

"You must not shed a tear, nor continue to fear,
That all men bring you such sorrow."

"Oh, really, is that what your wife thinks?"

YTHAN ESTUARY

*Skin tightens upon my bones
Like a claw. Not read yet in the runes,
I wonder how I am old and feel
Remorse and nostalgia fall
From my jaw.*

*Yet I remain silent. This hour is not
Meant for speech. Rather we should
Walk amidst the Northern Lights
On the estuary, where Canadian geese fly high,
Battling for a group, making us ask why they
To and fro in the dimming sun, looking for numbers,
Before they make their run: South, we imagine.*

Terrestrial, we walk on the beach.

*We may not have come and nearly the birds
Would have flown to an ignorant sand,
More empty without our grand gesture than it is
     now.*

*Fingers become cold and pink,
Trying in the late afternoon to think what we do:
What is best for me, for you.
Friends beckon, and we reckon on ending this trip to
   Ythan River's end.
Whatever the consequences, the sky on that day
Will say to me forever to listen—the Curlew's whistle,
The Cygnets' down brown and immature—
To love, without mention of mortality,
The sea at the estuary.*

G AND T

The mellow hours again,
From 6 to 7, when
Despite our wearying, travelling selves,
We relax on the train.

Standing-room only
Ended at Reading:
From Didcot on the bar
Dispensing

More rapidly, while
Rumbly-grumbly rocks
This tardy-heaped
Old rolling-stock.

The big smoke behind
For another day of
British Rail cancellations
And delay.

We make ourselves laugh,
While feeling quite chronic:
It's only amusing on the
Third Gin and Tonic!

TALK TO ME

Sometimes the conversation is parted
Before it's started.
You sit smugly, with your
Well-articulated views:
Far be it from me
To bring you some news.

Maybe, though, the world as you know it
Has other sights:
Different nights of dark and light.

I love you to talk, and I love to hear you.
But I will not fear you for not listening to me.

There might be something
That even you have not explored.
So, don't be floored,
When I ask you to ask me.
Why not just brave it and
Talk to me?

SACRED GEOMETRY

*As if I might remember now, my childhood soul
     anew,
I contemplate a sonnet song, to gently offer you.
Shakespeare intones in whispering haunt, from high
     up on the shelf,
Reminding me of magic days, when I could be my
     self.*

*I heard today of mystery—abstractions rare and
     true;
Of numbers swirling through our veins in blood of
     golden hue.
Fishermen hauling their heavy catch; farmers tilling
     the soil;
Scientists braving a virus batch; investors weighing
     their spoil;
Flamenco dancers bursting with sense; soldiers
     dying with none:
Amounting to more, and nothing less, than the
     lyrical number of one.*

*I shrank from the cosmos and hid for a while, for I
     didn't believe what I knew:
That the circle can square in a number of ways,
     obliging both me and you.
Holding us tight in the magical light, where music
     and science are twins,
Whose geometry balances perfectly, and neither
     loses nor wins.*